NAME

____

____

____

Name of Look ______________________

Evening ◯

Daytime ◯

Face

Moisturizer

Concealer

Foundation

Highlight/Blush

Eyes

Brows

Eyelid

Liner

Crease

Mascara

Lips

Liner

Lip Color

Gloss

Notes

Name of Look ______________________

Evening ○

Daytime ○

Face

Moisturizer

____

Concealer

____

Foundation

____

Highlight/Blush

____

Eyes

Brows

____

Eyelid

____

Liner

____

Crease

____

Mascara

____

Lips

Liner

____

Lip Color

____

Gloss

Notes

Name of Look _______________

Evening ◯

Daytime ◯

Face

Moisturizer

Concealer

Foundation

Highlight/Blush

Eyes

Brows

Eyelid

Liner

Crease

Mascara

Lips

Liner

Lip Color

Gloss

Notes

Name of Look _______________

Evening ◯
Daytime ◯

Face

Moisturizer

____

Concealer

____

Foundation

____

Highlight/Blush

____

Eyes

Brows

____

Eyelid

____

Liner

____

Crease

____

Mascara

____

Lips

Liner

____

Lip Color

____

Gloss

Notes

Name of Look _______________

Evening ○

Daytime ○

Face

Moisturizer

Concealer

Foundation

Highlight/Blush

Eyes

Brows

Eyelid

Liner

Crease

Mascara

Lips

Liner

Lip Color

Gloss

Notes

Name of Look __________________

Evening ○

Daytime ○

Face

Moisturizer
____

Concealer
____

Foundation
____

Highlight/Blush
____

Eyes

Brows
____

Eyelid
____

Liner
____

Crease
____

Mascara

Lips

Liner
____

Lip Color
____

Gloss

Notes

Name of Look ___________________

Evening ◯

Daytime ◯

Face

Moisturizer

____

Concealer

____

Foundation

____

Highlight/Blush

____

Eyes

Brows

____

Eyelid

____

Liner

____

Crease

____

Mascara

Lips

Liner

____

Lip Color

____

Gloss

____

Notes

Name of Look ___________________________

Evening ○

Daytime ○

Face

Moisturizer

____

Concealer

____

Foundation

____

Highlight/Blush

____

Eyes

Brows

____

Eyelid

____

Liner

____

Crease

____

Mascara

____

Lips

Liner

____

Lip Color

____

Gloss

____

Notes

Name of Look _______________

Evening ○

Daytime ○

Face

Moisturizer

Concealer

Foundation

Highlight/Blush

Eyes

Brows

Eyelid

Liner

Crease

Mascara

Lips

Liner

Lip Color

Gloss

Notes

Name of Look _______________

Evening ◯

Daytime ◯

Face

Moisturizer

____

Concealer

____

Foundation

____

Highlight/Blush

____

Eyes

Brows

____

Eyelid

____

Liner

____

Crease

____

Mascara

____

Lips

Liner

____

Lip Color

____

Gloss

____

Notes

Name of Look _______________

Evening ◯

Daytime ◯

Face

Moisturizer

____

Concealer

____

Foundation

____

Highlight/Blush

____

Eyes

Brows

____

Eyelid

____

Liner

____

Crease

____

Mascara

____

Lips

Liner

____

Lip Color

____

Gloss

____

Notes

Name of Look ___________________

Evening ◯

Daytime ◯

Face

Moisturizer

____

Concealer

____

Foundation

____

Highlight/Blush

____

Eyes

Brows

____

Eyelid

____

Liner

____

Crease

____

Mascara

____

Lips

Liner

____

Lip Color

____

Gloss

Notes

Name of Look _______________

Evening ◯

Daytime ◯

Face

Moisturizer

____

Concealer

____

Foundation

____

Highlight/Blush

____

Eyes

Brows

____

Eyelid

____

Liner

____

Crease

____

Mascara

Lips

Liner

____

Lip Color

____

Gloss

Notes

Name of Look ___________________

Evening ◯

Daytime ◯

Face

Moisturizer

____

Concealer

____

Foundation

____

Highlight/Blush

____

Eyes

Brows

____

Eyelid

Liner

____

Crease

____

Mascara

____

Lips

Liner

____

Lip Color

____

Gloss

____

Notes

Name of Look ___________________

Evening ○

Daytime ○

Face

Moisturizer

Concealer

Foundation

Highlight/Blush

Eyes

Brows

Eyelid

Liner

Crease

Mascara

Lips

Liner

Lip Color

Gloss

Notes

Name of Look _______________

Evening ○

Daytime ○

Face

Moisturizer

____

Concealer

____

Foundation

____

Highlight/Blush

____

Eyes

Brows

____

Eyelid

____

Liner

____

Crease

____

Mascara

____

Lips

Liner

____

Lip Color

____

Gloss

____

Notes

Name of Look ______________________

Evening ◯

Daytime ◯

Face

Moisturizer

____

Concealer

____

Foundation

____

Highlight/Blush

____

Eyes

Brows

____

Eyelid

____

Liner

____

Crease

____

Mascara

Lips

Liner

____

Lip Color

____

Gloss

Notes

Name of Look _______________

Evening ○

Daytime ○

Face

Moisturizer

____

Concealer

____

Foundation

____

Highlight/Blush

____

Eyes

Brows

____

Eyelid

____

Liner

____

Crease

____

Mascara

____

Lips

Liner

____

Lip Color

____

Gloss

Notes

Name of Look ___________________________

Evening ○

Daytime ○

Face

Moisturizer

Concealer

Foundation

Highlight/Blush

Eyes

Brows

Eyelid

Liner

Crease

Mascara

Lips

Liner

Lip Color

Gloss

Notes

Name of Look _______________________

Evening ◯

Daytime ◯

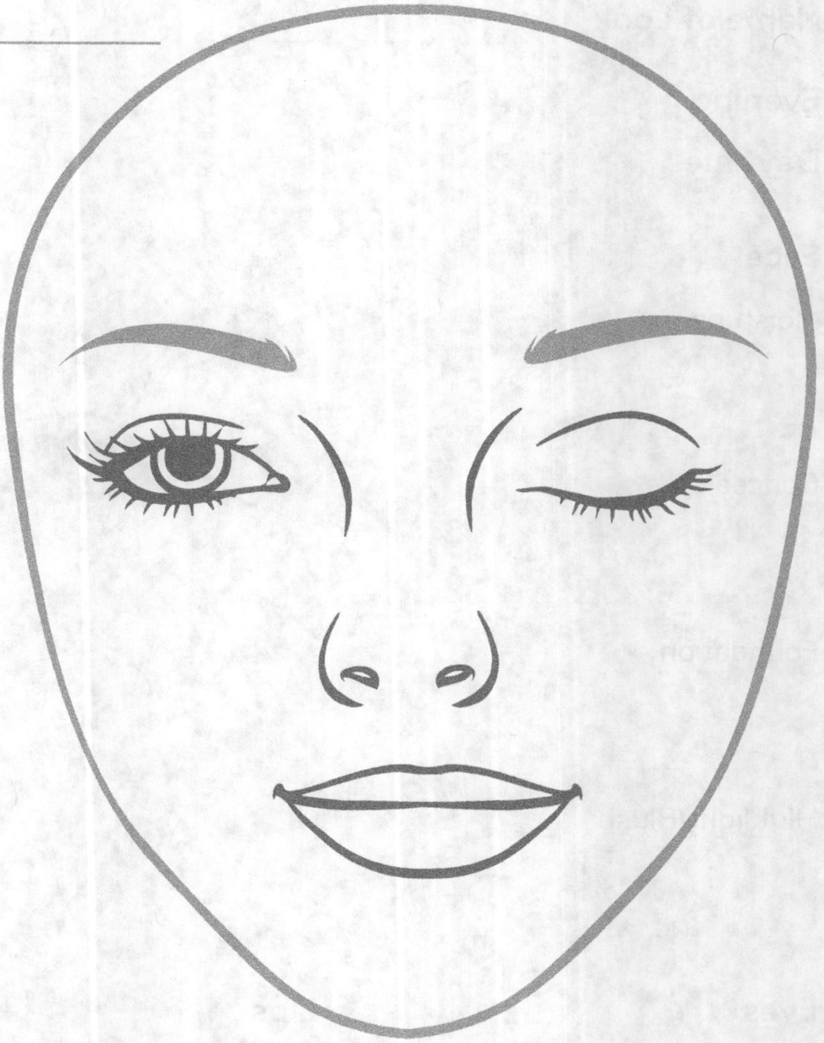

Face

Moisturizer

____

Concealer

____

Foundation

____

Highlight/Blush

____

Eyes

Brows

____

Eyelid

____

Liner

____

Crease

____

Mascara

____

Lips

Liner

____

Lip Color

____

Gloss

____

Notes

Name of Look ______________________

Evening ◯

Daytime ◯

Face

Moisturizer

Concealer

Foundation

Highlight/Blush

Eyes

Brows

Eyelid

Liner

Crease

Mascara

Lips

Liner

Lip Color

Gloss

Notes

Name of Look _______________________

Evening ○

Daytime ○

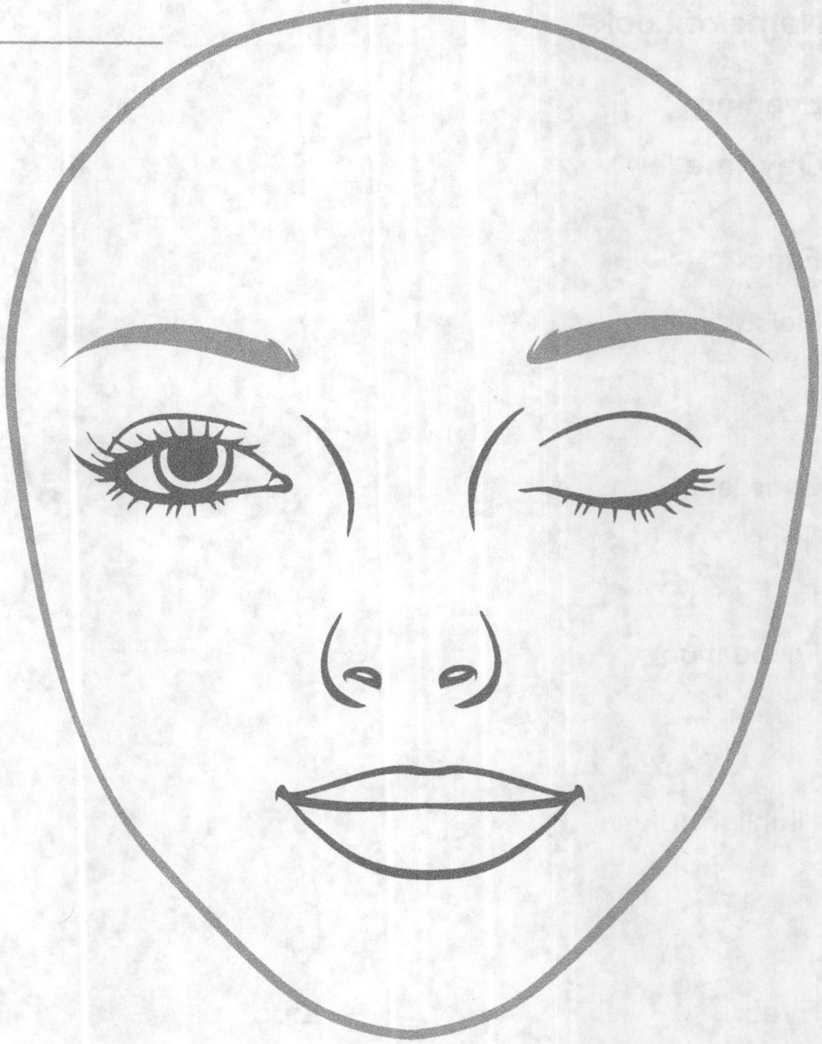

Face

Moisturizer

____

Concealer

____

Foundation

____

Highlight/Blush

____

Eyes

Brows

____

Eyelid

____

Liner

____

Crease

____

Mascara

____

Lips

Liner

____

Lip Color

____

Gloss

____

Notes

Name of Look _______________

Evening ◯

Daytime ◯

Face

Moisturizer

____

Concealer

____

Foundation

____

Highlight/Blush

____

Eyes

Brows

____

Eyelid

____

Liner

____

Crease

____

Mascara

____

Lips

Liner

____

Lip Color

____

Gloss

____

Notes

Name of Look _______________________

Evening ◯

Daytime ◯

Face

Moisturizer

____

Concealer

____

Foundation

____

Highlight/Blush

____

Eyes

Brows

____

Eyelid

____

Liner

____

Crease

____

Mascara

____

Lips

Liner

____

Lip Color

____

Gloss

Notes

Name of Look ___________________________

Evening ◯

Daytime ◯

Face

Moisturizer

____

Concealer

____

Foundation

____

Highlight/Blush

____

Eyes

Brows

____

Eyelid

____

Liner

____

Crease

____

Mascara

____

Lips

Liner

____

Lip Color

____

Gloss

Notes

Name of Look ______________________

Evening ◯

Daytime ◯

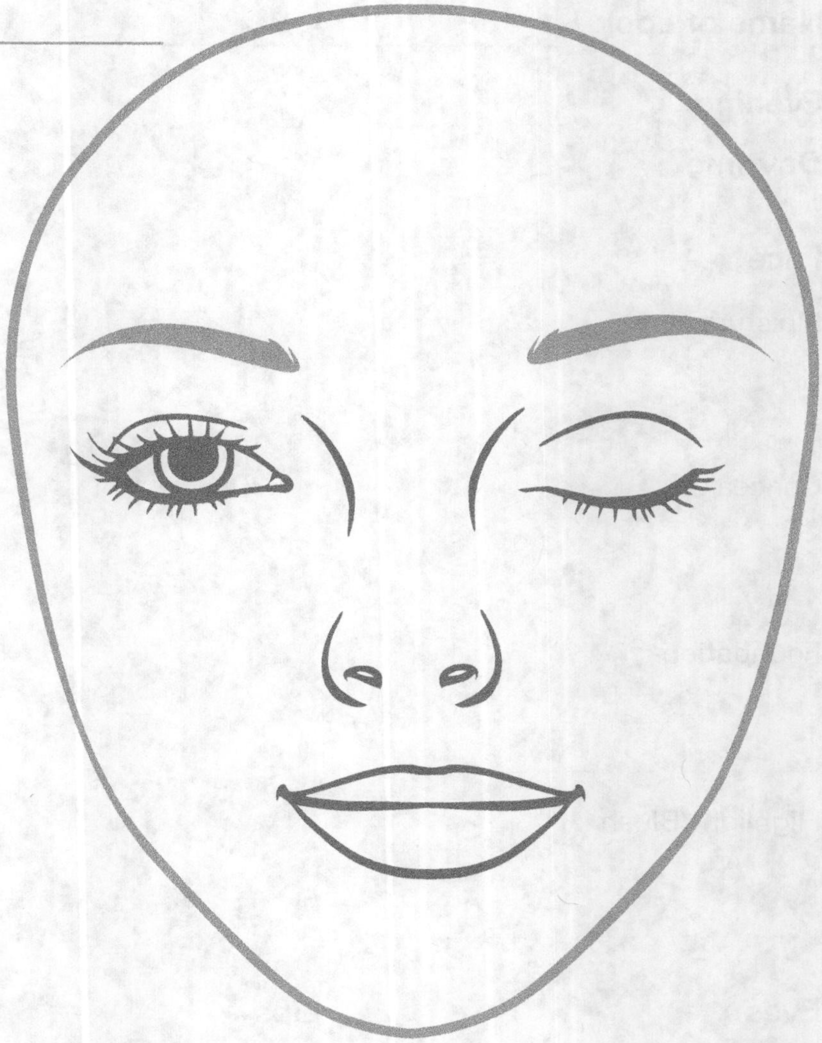

Face

Moisturizer

____

Concealer

____

Foundation

____

Highlight/Blush

____

Eyes

Brows

____

Eyelid

____

Liner

____

Crease

____

Mascara

Lips

Liner

____

Lip Color

____

Gloss

Notes

Name of Look ______________________

Evening ◯

Daytime ◯

Face

Moisturizer

____

Concealer

____

Foundation

____

Highlight/Blush

____

Eyes

Brows

____

Eyelid

____

Liner

____

Crease

____

Mascara

Lips

Liner

____

Lip Color

____

Gloss

____

Notes

Name of Look ______________________

Evening ◯

Daytime ◯

Face

Moisturizer

____

Concealer

____

Foundation

____

Highlight/Blush

____

Eyes

Brows

____

Eyelid

____

Liner

____

Crease

____

Mascara

____

Lips

Liner

____

Lip Color

____

Gloss

____

Notes

Name of Look ___________________________

Evening ◯

Daytime ◯

Face

Moisturizer

Concealer

Foundation

Highlight/Blush

Eyes

Brows

Eyelid

Liner

Crease

Mascara

Lips

Liner

Lip Color

Gloss

Notes

Name of Look ______________________

Evening ◯

Daytime ◯

Face

Moisturizer

____

Concealer

____

Foundation

____

Highlight/Blush

____

Eyes

Brows

____

Eyelid

____

Liner

____

Crease

____

Mascara

Lips

Liner

____

Lip Color

____

Gloss

Notes

Name of Look _______________

Evening ◯

Daytime ◯

Face

Moisturizer

Concealer

Foundation

Highlight/Blush

Eyes

Brows

Eyelid

Liner

Crease

Mascara

Lips

Liner

Lip Color

Gloss

Notes

Name of Look ___________________________

Evening ○
Daytime ○

Face

Moisturizer

____

Concealer

____

Foundation

____

Highlight/Blush

____

Eyes

Brows

____

Eyelid

____

Liner

____

Crease

____

Mascara

____

Lips

Liner

____

Lip Color

____

Gloss

____

Notes

Name of Look _______________

Evening ◯

Daytime ◯

Face

Moisturizer

____

Concealer

____

Foundation

____

Highlight/Blush

____

Eyes

Brows

____

Eyelid

____

Liner

____

Crease

____

Mascara

Lips

Liner

____

Lip Color

____

Gloss

Notes

Name of Look _______________

Evening ◯

Daytime ◯

Face

Moisturizer

____

Concealer

____

Foundation

____

Highlight/Blush

____

Eyes

Brows

____

Eyelid

____

Liner

____

Crease

____

Mascara

____

Lips

Liner

____

Lip Color

____

Gloss

____

Notes

Name of Look ______________________________

Evening ⚪

Daytime ⚪

Face

Moisturizer

Concealer

Foundation

Highlight/Blush

Eyes

Brows

Eyelid

Liner

Crease

Mascara

Lips

Liner

Lip Color

Gloss

Notes

Name of Look _______________________

Evening ○

Daytime ○

Face

Moisturizer

____

Concealer

____

Foundation

____

Highlight/Blush

____

Eyes

Brows

____

Eyelid

____

Liner

____

Crease

____

Mascara

____

Lips

Liner

____

Lip Color

____

Gloss

____

Notes

Name of Look

Evening ○

Daytime ○

Face

Moisturizer

Concealer

Foundation

Highlight/Blush

Eyes

Brows

Eyelid

Liner

Crease

Mascara

Lips

Liner

Lip Color

Gloss

Notes

Name of Look _______________

Evening ◯

Daytime ◯

Face

Moisturizer

Concealer

Foundation

Highlight/Blush

Eyes

Brows

Eyelid

Liner

Crease

Mascara

Lips

Liner

Lip Color

Gloss

Notes

Name of Look _______________

Evening ◯

Daytime ◯

Face

Moisturizer

Concealer

Foundation

Highlight/Blush

Eyes

Brows

Eyelid

Liner

Crease

Mascara

Lips

Liner

Lip Color

Gloss

Notes

Name of Look ______________________

Evening ◯

Daytime ◯

Face

Moisturizer

____

Concealer

____

Foundation

____

Highlight/Blush

____

Eyes

Brows

____

Eyelid

____

Liner

____

Crease

____

Mascara

____

Lips

Liner

____

Lip Color

____

Gloss

____

Notes

Name of Look _______________

Evening ◯

Daytime ◯

Face

Moisturizer

____

Concealer

____

Foundation

____

Highlight/Blush

____

Eyes

Brows

____

Eyelid

____

Liner

____

Crease

____

Mascara

____

Lips

Liner

____

Lip Color

____

Gloss

____

Notes

Name of Look _______________________

Evening ◯

Daytime ◯

Face

Moisturizer

____

Concealer

____

Foundation

____

Highlight/Blush

____

Eyes

Brows

____

Eyelid

____

Liner

____

Crease

____

Mascara

Lips

Liner

____

Lip Color

____

Gloss

Notes

Name of Look _______________

Evening ◯

Daytime ◯

Face

Moisturizer

Concealer

Foundation

Highlight/Blush

Eyes

Brows

Eyelid

Liner

Crease

Mascara

Lips

Liner

Lip Color

Gloss

Notes

Name of Look ______________________

Evening ◯

Daytime ◯

Face

Moisturizer

____

Concealer

____

Foundation

____

Highlight/Blush

____

Eyes

Brows

____

Eyelid

____

Liner

____

Crease

____

Mascara

Lips

Liner

____

Lip Color

____

Gloss

____

Notes

Name of Look _______________

Evening ○
Daytime ○

Face

Moisturizer

Concealer

Foundation

Highlight/Blush

Eyes

Brows

Eyelid

Liner

Crease

Mascara

Lips

Liner

Lip Color

Gloss

Notes

Name of Look ______________________

Evening ○
Daytime ○

Face

Moisturizer
____

Concealer
____

Foundation
____

Highlight/Blush
____

Eyes

Brows
____

Eyelid
____

Liner
____

Crease
____

Mascara

Lips

Liner
____

Lip Color
____

Gloss

Notes

Name of Look _______________

Evening ○

Daytime ○

Face

Moisturizer

Concealer

Foundation

Highlight/Blush

Eyes

Brows

Eyelid

Liner

Crease

Mascara

Lips

Liner

Lip Color

Gloss

Notes

Name of Look _______________

Evening ◯

Daytime ◯

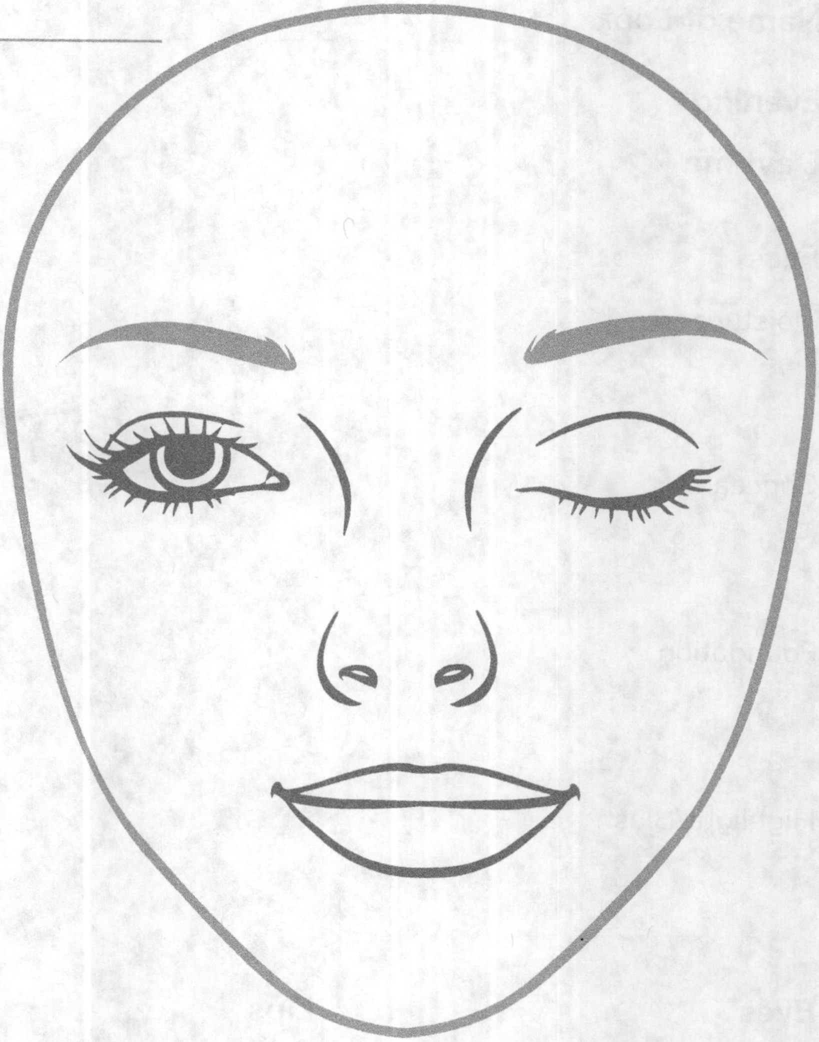

Face

Moisturizer

____

Concealer

____

Foundation

____

Highlight/Blush

____

Eyes

Brows

____

Eyelid

____

Liner

____

Crease

____

Mascara

____

Lips

Liner

____

Lip Color

____

Gloss

____

Notes

Name of Look ___________________

Evening ◯

Daytime ◯

Face

Moisturizer

Concealer

Foundation

Highlight/Blush

Eyes

Brows

Eyelid

Liner

Crease

Mascara

Lips

Liner

Lip Color

Gloss

Notes

Name of Look ______________________

Evening ◯

Daytime ◯

Face

Moisturizer

____

Concealer

____

Foundation

____

Highlight/Blush

____

Eyes

Brows

____

Eyelid

____

Liner

____

Crease

____

Mascara

____

Lips

Liner

____

Lip Color

____

Gloss

____

Notes

Name of Look ______________________

Evening ◯

Daytime ◯

Face

Moisturizer

____

Concealer

____

Foundation

____

Highlight/Blush

____

Eyes

Brows

____

Eyelid

____

Liner

____

Crease

____

Mascara

____

Lips

Liner

____

Lip Color

____

Gloss

____

Notes

Name of Look _______________

Evening ◯

Daytime ◯

Face

Moisturizer

____

Concealer

____

Foundation

____

Highlight/Blush

____

Eyes

Brows

____

Eyelid

____

Liner

____

Crease

____

Mascara

____

Lips

Liner

____

Lip Color

____

Gloss

____

Notes

Name of Look ___________________________

Evening ○

Daytime ○

Face

Moisturizer

____

Concealer

____

Foundation

____

Highlight/Blush

____

Eyes

Brows

____

Eyelid

____

Liner

____

Crease

____

Mascara

Lips

Liner

____

Lip Color

____

Gloss

Notes

Name of Look ______________________

Evening ⚪
Daytime ⚪

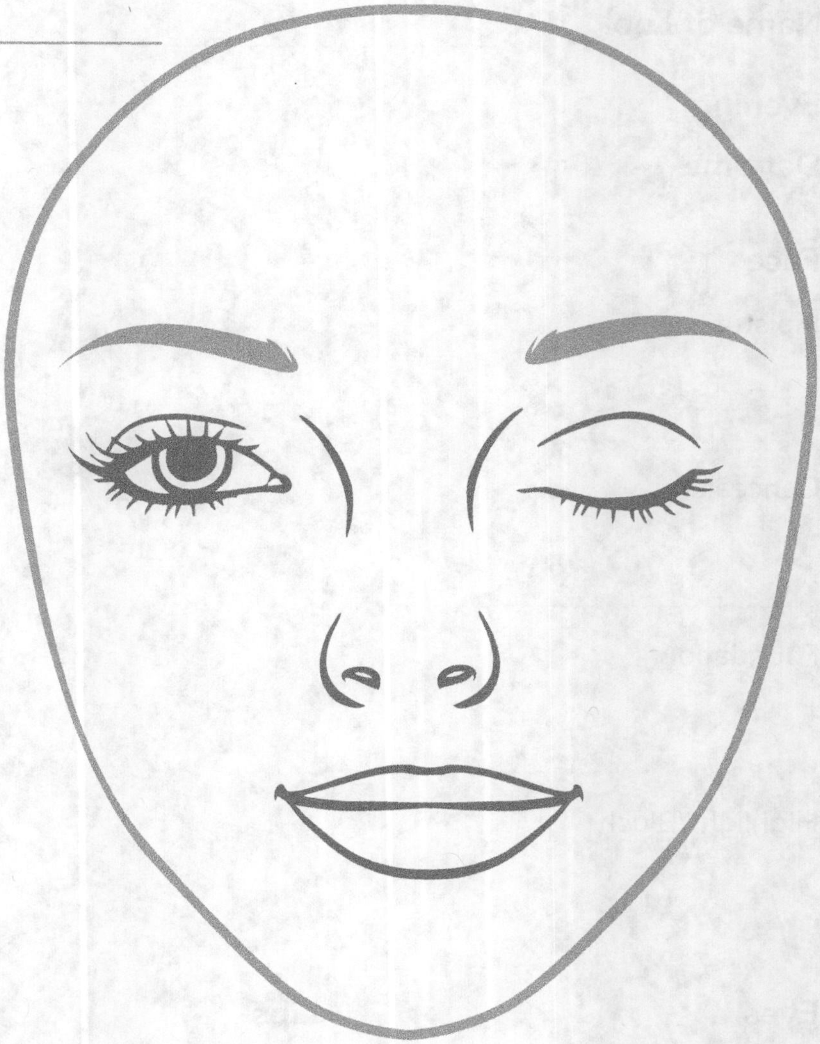

Face
Moisturizer

____

Concealer

____

Foundation

____

Highlight/Blush

____

Eyes

Brows

____

Eyelid

____

Liner

____

Crease

____

Mascara

Lips

Liner

____

Lip Color

____

Gloss

Notes

Name of Look _________________________

Evening ○

Daytime ○

Face

Moisturizer

Concealer

Foundation

Highlight/Blush

Eyes

Brows

Eyelid

Liner

Crease

Mascara

Lips

Liner

Lip Color

Gloss

Notes

Name of Look

Evening ○

Daytime ○

Face

Moisturizer

Concealer

Foundation

Highlight/Blush

Eyes

Brows

Eyelid

Liner

Crease

Mascara

Lips

Liner

Lip Color

Gloss

Notes

Name of Look _______________

Evening ◯

Daytime ◯

Face

Moisturizer

____

Concealer

____

Foundation

____

Highlight/Blush

____

Eyes

Brows

____

Eyelid

____

Liner

____

Crease

____

Mascara

Lips

Liner

____

Lip Color

____

Gloss

____

Notes

Name of Look ___________________

Evening ○

Daytime ○

Face

Moisturizer

Concealer

Foundation

Highlight/Blush

Eyes

Brows

Eyelid

Liner

Crease

Mascara

Lips

Liner

Lip Color

Gloss

Notes

Name of Look ___________________

Evening ○

Daytime ○

Face

Moisturizer

____

Concealer

____

Foundation

____

Highlight/Blush

____

Eyes

Brows

____

Eyelid

____

Liner

____

Crease

____

Mascara

____

Lips

Liner

____

Lip Color

____

Gloss

____

Notes

Name of Look ___________________

Evening ◯

Daytime ◯

Face

Moisturizer

____

Concealer

____

Foundation

____

Highlight/Blush

____

Eyes

Brows

____

Eyelid

____

Liner

____

Crease

____

Mascara

____

Lips

Liner

____

Lip Color

____

Gloss

____

Notes

Name of Look

Evening ○

Daytime ○

Face

Moisturizer

Concealer

Foundation

Highlight/Blush

Eyes

Brows

Eyelid

Liner

Crease

Mascara

Lips

Liner

Lip Color

Gloss

Notes

Name of Look ______________________

Evening ○

Daytime ○

Face

Moisturizer

____

Concealer

____

Foundation

____

Highlight/Blush

____

Eyes

Brows

____

Eyelid

____

Liner

____

Crease

____

Mascara

____

Lips

Liner

____

Lip Color

____

Gloss

____

Notes

Name of Look ___________________

Evening ○

Daytime ○

Face

Moisturizer

Concealer

Foundation

Highlight/Blush

Eyes

Brows

Eyelid

Liner

Crease

Mascara

Lips

Liner

Lip Color

Gloss

Notes

Name of Look _______________

Evening ◯

Daytime ◯

Face

Moisturizer

Concealer

Foundation

Highlight/Blush

Eyes

Brows

Eyelid

Liner

Crease

Mascara

Lips

Liner

Lip Color

Gloss

Notes

Name of Look _______________

Evening ○

Daytime ○

Face

Moisturizer

Concealer

Foundation

Highlight/Blush

Eyes

Brows

Eyelid

Liner

Crease

Mascara

Lips

Liner

Lip Color

Gloss

Notes

Name of Look ______________________

Evening ◯

Daytime ◯

Face

Moisturizer

____

Concealer

____

Foundation

____

Highlight/Blush

____

Eyes

Brows

____

Eyelid

____

Liner

____

Crease

____

Mascara

____

Lips

Liner

____

Lip Color

____

Gloss

Notes

Name of Look _______________

Evening ◯

Daytime ◯

Face

Moisturizer

____

Concealer

____

Foundation

____

Highlight/Blush

____

Eyes

Brows

____

Eyelid

____

Liner

____

Crease

____

Mascara

Lips

Liner

____

Lip Color

____

Gloss

Notes

Name of Look _______________________

Evening ◯

Daytime ◯

Face

Moisturizer

____

Concealer

____

Foundation

____

Highlight/Blush

____

Eyes

Brows

____

Eyelid

____

Liner

____

Crease

____

Mascara

____

Lips

Liner

____

Lip Color

____

Gloss

____

Notes

Name of Look ___________________

Evening ○

Daytime ○

Face

Moisturizer

Concealer

Foundation

Highlight/Blush

Eyes

Brows

Eyelid

Liner

Crease

Mascara

Lips

Liner

Lip Color

Gloss

Notes

Name of Look ___________________

Evening ◯

Daytime ◯

Face

Moisturizer

Concealer

Foundation

Highlight/Blush

Eyes

Brows

Eyelid

Liner

Crease

Mascara

Lips

Liner

Lip Color

Gloss

Notes

Name of Look ______________________

Evening ◯

Daytime ◯

Face

Moisturizer

____

Concealer

____

Foundation

____

Highlight/Blush

____

Eyes

Brows

____

Eyelid

____

Liner

____

Crease

____

Mascara

____

Lips

Liner

____

Lip Color

____

Gloss

____

Notes

Name of Look _______________________

Evening ◯

Daytime ◯

Face

Moisturizer

____

Concealer

____

Foundation

____

Highlight/Blush

____

Eyes

Brows

____

Eyelid

____

Liner

____

Crease

____

Mascara

____

Lips

Liner

____

Lip Color

____

Gloss

____

Notes

Name of Look ______________________

Evening ⚪

Daytime ⚪

Face

Moisturizer

Concealer

Foundation

Highlight/Blush

Eyes

Brows

Eyelid

Liner

Crease

Mascara

Lips

Liner

Lip Color

Gloss

Notes

Name of Look _______________________

Evening ◯

Daytime ◯

Face

Moisturizer

____

Concealer

____

Foundation

____

Highlight/Blush

____

Eyes

Brows

____

Eyelid

____

Liner

____

Crease

____

Mascara

____

Lips

Liner

____

Lip Color

____

Gloss

____

Notes

Name of Look _________________________

Evening ○
Daytime ○

Face

Moisturizer

____

Concealer

____

Foundation

____

Highlight/Blush

____

Eyes

Brows

____

Eyelid

____

Liner

____

Crease

____

Mascara

Lips

Liner

____

Lip Color

____

Gloss

____

Notes

Name of Look _______________________

Evening ○

Daytime ○

Face

Moisturizer
____

Concealer
____

Foundation
____

Highlight/Blush
____

Eyes

Brows
____

Eyelid
____

Liner
____

Crease
____

Mascara
____

Lips

Liner
____

Lip Color
____

Gloss
____

Notes

Name of Look ___________________

Evening ◯

Daytime ◯

Face

Moisturizer

Concealer

Foundation

Highlight/Blush

Eyes

Brows

Eyelid

Liner

Crease

Mascara

Lips

Liner

Lip Color

Gloss

Notes

Name of Look _______________

Evening ◯

Daytime ◯

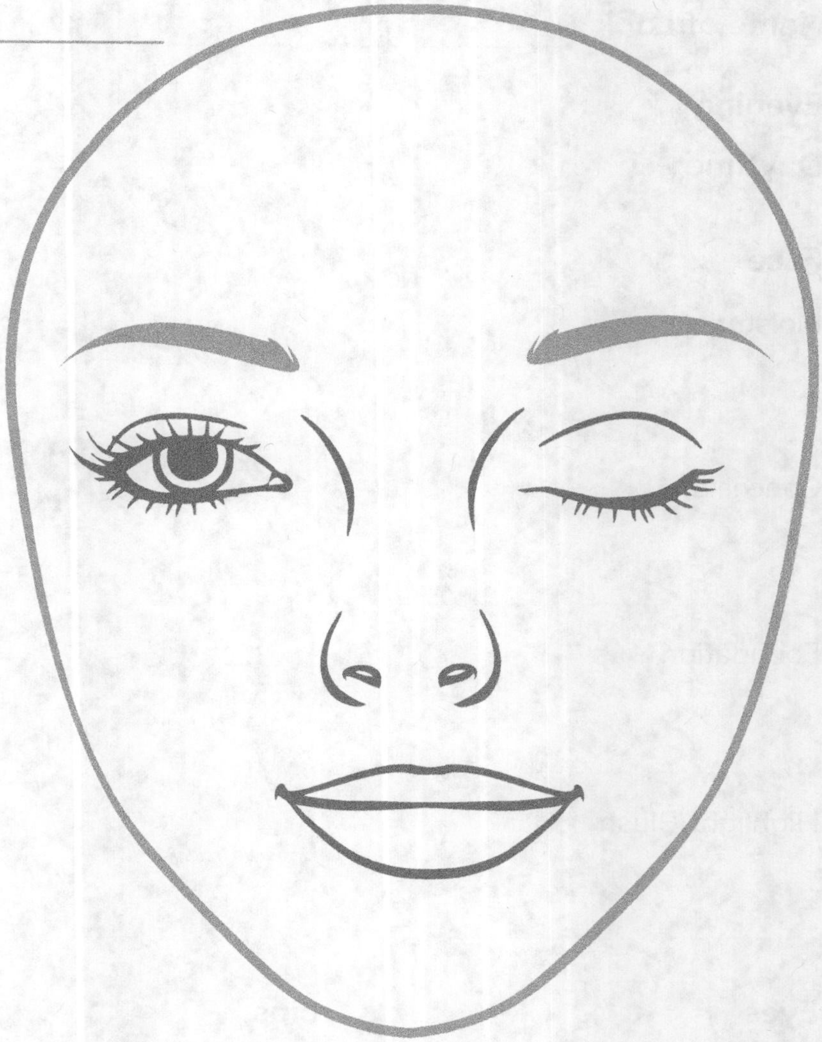

Face

Moisturizer
____

Concealer
____

Foundation
____

Highlight/Blush
____

Eyes

Brows
____

Eyelid
____

Liner
____

Crease
____

Mascara

Lips

Liner
____

Lip Color
____

Gloss

Notes

Name of Look ___________________

Evening ○

Daytime ○

Face

Moisturizer

Concealer

Foundation

Highlight/Blush

Eyes

Brows

Eyelid

Liner

Crease

Mascara

Lips

Liner

Lip Color

Gloss

Notes

Name of Look ______________________

Evening ◯

Daytime ◯

Face

Moisturizer

____

Concealer

____

Foundation

____

Highlight/Blush

____

Eyes

Brows

____

Eyelid

____

Liner

____

Crease

____

Mascara

____

Lips

Liner

____

Lip Color

____

Gloss

____

Notes

Name of Look _______________________

Evening ◯

Daytime ◯

Face

Moisturizer

Concealer

Foundation

Highlight/Blush

Eyes

Brows

Eyelid

Liner

Crease

Mascara

Lips

Liner

Lip Color

Gloss

Notes

Name of Look ___________________

Evening ◯

Daytime ◯

Face

Moisturizer

____

Concealer

____

Foundation

____

Highlight/Blush

____

Eyes

Brows

____

Eyelid

____

Liner

____

Crease

____

Mascara

____

Lips

Liner

____

Lip Color

____

Gloss

Notes

Name of Look _______________

Evening ◯

Daytime ◯

Face

Moisturizer

Concealer

Foundation

Highlight/Blush

Eyes

Brows

Eyelid

Liner

Crease

Mascara

Lips

Liner

Lip Color

Gloss

Notes

Name of Look ___________________

Evening ○

Daytime ○

Face

Moisturizer

____

Concealer

____

Foundation

____

Highlight/Blush

____

Eyes

Brows

____

Eyelid

____

Liner

____

Crease

____

Mascara

____

Lips

Liner

____

Lip Color

____

Gloss

____

Notes

Name of Look _______________

Evening ◯

Daytime ◯

Face

Moisturizer

Concealer

Foundation

Highlight/Blush

Eyes

Brows

Eyelid

Liner

Crease

Mascara

Lips

Liner

Lip Color

Gloss

Notes

Name of Look _______________

Evening ○

Daytime ○

Face

Moisturizer

____

Concealer

____

Foundation

____

Highlight/Blush

____

Eyes

Brows

____

Eyelid

____

Liner

____

Crease

____

Mascara

____

Lips

Liner

____

Lip Color

____

Gloss

____

Notes

Name of Look ______________________

Evening ◯

Daytime ◯

Face

Moisturizer

____

Concealer

____

Foundation

____

Highlight/Blush

____

Eyes

Brows

____

Eyelid

____

Liner

____

Crease

____

Mascara

Lips

Liner

____

Lip Color

____

Gloss

____

Notes

Name of Look _______________________

Evening ◯

Daytime ◯

Face

Moisturizer

____

Concealer

____

Foundation

____

Highlight/Blush

____

Eyes

Brows

____

Eyelid

____

Liner

____

Crease

____

Mascara

Lips

Liner

____

Lip Color

____

Gloss

____

Notes

Name of Look _______________________

Evening ◯

Daytime ◯

Face

Moisturizer

____

Concealer

____

Foundation

____

Highlight/Blush

____

Eyes

Brows

____

Eyelid

____

Liner

____

Crease

____

Mascara

Lips

Liner

____

Lip Color

____

Gloss

Notes

Name of Look _______________

Evening ◯

Daytime ◯

Face

Moisturizer

____

Concealer

____

Foundation

____

Highlight/Blush

____

Eyes

Brows

____

Eyelid

____

Liner

____

Crease

____

Mascara

____

Lips

Liner

____

Lip Color

____

Gloss

____

Notes

Name of Look ______________________

Evening ◯

Daytime ◯

Face

Moisturizer

Concealer

Foundation

Highlight/Blush

Eyes

Brows

Eyelid

Liner

Crease

Mascara

Lips

Liner

Lip Color

Gloss

Notes

Name of Look _______________________

Evening ◯
Daytime ◯

Face

Moisturizer

____

Concealer

____

Foundation

____

Highlight/Blush

____

Eyes

Brows

____

Eyelid

____

Liner

____

Crease

____

Mascara

____

Lips

Liner

____

Lip Color

____

Gloss

____

Notes

Name of Look _______________________

Evening ◯

Daytime ◯

Face

Moisturizer

Concealer

Foundation

Highlight/Blush

Eyes

Brows

Eyelid

Liner

Crease

Mascara

Lips

Liner

Lip Color

Gloss

Notes

Name of Look _______________

Evening ◯
Daytime ◯

Face

Moisturizer

____

Concealer

____

Foundation

____

Highlight/Blush

____

Eyes

Brows

____

Eyelid

____

Liner

____

Crease

____

Mascara

Lips

Liner

____

Lip Color

____

Gloss

Notes

Name of Look ______________________

Evening ○

Daytime ○

Face

Moisturizer

Concealer

Foundation

Highlight/Blush

Eyes

Brows

Eyelid

Liner

Crease

Mascara

Lips

Liner

Lip Color

Gloss

Notes

Name of Look _______________________

Evening ○
Daytime ○

Face

Moisturizer

____

Concealer

____

Foundation

____

Highlight/Blush

____

Eyes

Brows

____

Eyelid

____

Liner

____

Crease

____

Mascara

Lips

Liner

____

Lip Color

____

Gloss

Notes

Name of Look ___________________________

Evening ○

Daytime ○

Face

Moisturizer

Concealer

Foundation

Highlight/Blush

Eyes

Brows

Eyelid

Liner

Crease

Mascara

Lips

Liner

Lip Color

Gloss

Notes

Name of Look ___________________

Evening ◯

Daytime ◯

Face

Moisturizer

____

Concealer

____

Foundation

____

Highlight/Blush

____

Eyes

Brows

____

Eyelid

____

Liner

____

Crease

____

Mascara

Lips

Liner

____

Lip Color

____

Gloss

Notes

Name of Look _______________

Evening ◯
Daytime ◯

Face

Moisturizer

Concealer

Foundation

Highlight/Blush

Eyes

Brows

Eyelid

Liner

Crease

Mascara

Lips

Liner

Lip Color

Gloss

Notes

Name of Look ___________________

Evening ◯

Daytime ◯

Face

Moisturizer

____

Concealer

____

Foundation

____

Highlight/Blush

____

Eyes

Brows

____

Eyelid

____

Liner

____

Crease

____

Mascara

____

Lips

Liner

____

Lip Color

____

Gloss

____

Notes

Name of Look ______________________

Evening ◯

Daytime ◯

Face

Moisturizer

____

Concealer

____

Foundation

____

Highlight/Blush

____

Eyes

Brows

____

Eyelid

____

Liner

____

Crease

____

Mascara

Lips

Liner

____

Lip Color

____

Gloss

Notes

Name of Look _______________

Evening ○

Daytime ○

Face

Moisturizer
____

Concealer
____

Foundation
____

Highlight/Blush
____

Eyes

Brows
____

Eyelid
____

Liner
____

Crease
____

Mascara
____

Lips

Liner
____

Lip Color
____

Gloss
____

Notes

Name of Look _______________

Evening ○
Daytime ○

Face

Moisturizer

Concealer

Foundation

Highlight/Blush

Eyes

Brows

Eyelid

Liner

Crease

Mascara

Lips

Liner

Lip Color

Gloss

Notes

Name of Look

Evening ○
Daytime ○

Face

Moisturizer

Concealer

Foundation

Highlight/Blush

Eyes

Brows

Eyelid

Liner

Crease

Mascara

Lips

Liner

Lip Color

Gloss

Notes

Name of Look _______________

Evening ◯

Daytime ◯

Face

Moisturizer
____

Concealer
____

Foundation
____

Highlight/Blush
____

Eyes

Brows
____

Eyelid
____

Liner
____

Crease
____

Mascara

Lips

Liner
____

Lip Color
____

Gloss
____

Notes

Name of Look ___________________

Evening ◯

Daytime ◯

Face

Moisturizer

Concealer

Foundation

Highlight/Blush

Eyes

Brows

Eyelid

Liner

Crease

Mascara

Lips

Liner

Lip Color

Gloss

Notes

Name of Look ____________________

Evening ○

Daytime ○

Face

Moisturizer

Concealer

Foundation

Highlight/Blush

Eyes

Brows

Eyelid

Liner

Crease

Mascara

Lips

Liner

Lip Color

Gloss

Notes

Name of Look _______________________

Evening ◯

Daytime ◯

Face

Moisturizer

____

Concealer

____

Foundation

____

Highlight/Blush

____

Eyes

Brows

____

Eyelid

____

Liner

____

Crease

____

Mascara

Lips

Liner

____

Lip Color

____

Gloss

Notes

9 798611 854891